the flap pamphlet series

A Warning to the House That Holds Me

open, read, turn

A Warning to the House that holds me

the flap pamphlet series (No. 19)

Published by the flap series, 2019
the pamphlet series of flipped eye publishing
All Rights Reserved

Cover Design by Petraski
Series Design © flipped eye publishing, 2010

Author Photo © Aiden Hamitt Williams
First Edition
Copyright © Amina Jama 2019

ISBN-13: 978-1-905233-57-1

For Aabo and Ayeeyo Halimo

A Warning to the House That Holds Me

by Amina Jama

Contents | *A Warning to the House That Holds Me*

Context

Part one. *Magdalena Carmen Frida Kahlo y Calderon is born on July 6 in Coyoacan, then a suburb of Mexico City.*

Later in life she claims July 7, 1910, as her birthday, in solidarity with the Mexican Revolution.

Part two. *In 1925, Kahlo is riding in a bus that is hit by a streetcar. She is pierced by a metal handrail and suffers extensive spinal and pelvic fractures, broken ribs and a broken foot.*

The effects of the injuries plague her throughout her life. During her recovery, she begins to paint and meets Diego Rivera.

They marry, and she resigns from the Communist Party after he is expelled.

Part three. *In 1930 Rivera and Kahlo move to San Francisco.*

By 1934 Kahlo cuts off her hair after discovering Rivera is having an affair with her sister Cristina.

After leaving Rivera, she sells her first paintings and showcases her first solo exhibition in New York.

Part four. *In 1950, Kahlo is hospitalized for nearly a year in Mexico City. The following year she is confined to a wheelchair with full-time nursing care.*

In 1953, Kahlo's leg is amputated.
She also showcases her first solo exhibition in Mexico. Kahlo attends the opening in her bed.

Part five. *After Frida Kahlo passes, Diego Rivera locks all of Frida's belongings in the bathroom of Casa Azul, ordering it to be opened fifty years after her death.*

Shortly before she dies, she writes, "I hope the exit is joyful — and I hope never to come back — Frida."

five

self-portrait of an ageing mother
After Safia Elhillo

i lost my mother to her sons.
hooyo raised her boys with all the love she has ever been taught,

then raised her daughters with whatever she had left over.
i left hooyo in ███████████, she discovered her body;

now passing minutes are the only thing she trusts
and she never lets me forget it. i ask her

███████████, she replies *i'm exactly where you left me.*
to be old and fleeing. to be young and boarding.

to be old and losing everything you voted for.
her hands cup her ██ tighter, when there is any mention of home,

crumbling it in her fingers like the sun going down.
qalbiyay toos. to see your body losing you in the mirror   a tangible feeling

you can't delay   the last ██ times i saw her she updates me
on her ██ condition   says
my body is giving up on me and growing one of its own.

she covers her face in haba suud until the burning stops,
until the sun goes down.

i lost hooyo to ███████, i lost ██████████.
she calls me once or ████████ a day, just to ask if i've eaten.

to see if i picked my skin off the bed in the morning.
to be ██████████ and ██████████

is what it means to be able to walk
in any direction you want.

9

when I say that loving me is kind of like being an england football fan

After Hanif Abdurraqib

what i mean is, it isn't easy, what i mean is
you can't bring yourself to supplicate
on my behalf - even when i write it down for you,
tell you to repeat after me.

on loving me, there is a *buur*
of crumbled cigarette papers gathering dust
in the corners of the country you left,
the one no one returns to.

look at all of these moments of love:
a display of photo frames i am not in,
trophies i never won.
you might ask why i return every four years?
i'll say *i just woke up one day*
and there was a sheet of lonely over my body, no one
has since bothered to take it off.

i want to say, *of course i love myself* but there is
no way to prove it.

on loving me, i might say *i promise, i promise*
my heart just needs a change of seasons and
then i will be alive again.

then i will say
loving me is kind of like searching for air in
a heatwave. the weather warning suggests you
stay indoors.

someday i'll love amina jama
After Frank O'Hara/ After Roger Reeves/ After Ocean Vuong

amina,
if you're reading this then you've finally given in
to the whispers. you've renamed yourself *nobody.*
though it's traditional to be poised and waxed,
you're not.

you dip the tips of your fingers in red henna, like
the night you climbed out of bed and gathered yourself
in the sheets. i promised to never tell anyone, i'm sorry.

amina,
you've given up impressing her, your hands
catching the air with gestures. catching the cars before they hit.
no one can take that
fight from you. do you hear it?
the fire in your chest. *let it burn.*

amina,
you spent months planning
the janazah that will rival all.
you found a way to carry yourself in.

amina,
twitter has taken over the 10 o'clock news,
announcing that borders have street names.
the one you left him on is named *astagfirullah.*

amina,
when they left, the world spun around
like candy floss,
then melts under water like black.

11

application for motherhood

i.   frida is in a pool of her own blood.
she never makes it to 40 weeks,
never heard the words full term,
never had twin gravestones,
nor a man to hold her down like she did him.

ii.   *my painting carries with it the message of pain.*

iii.   frida,
can i call you frida?
i've been doing it so far.

in the end, you
tried to drown my sorrows
but the damned things learnt how to swim.

you locked your life away in the bathroom
of casa azul. half a century later, we opened
to found you lying clutching letters.
you built *walls around your sadness,*
stopping it from devouring you from the inside.

but frida, what about your dresses?
you left them to fend for themselves
against diego. you left us to clean the floor
and put your face on postcards for the world to consume.

wild geese

After Mary Oliver / After Hera Lindsay Bird

you do not have to be good,
is what they tell you when you are already under their thumb.
when life and energy have already left your body.
you: malleable, mouldable, exhausted.

you do not have to walk on your knees,
for a hundred miles through the desert, repenting.
even in death, forgive them nothing.
even your valley of glee, you take off

your hijab and twerk in the mosque.
your glutes pointed towards the qibla. you do not have to try
so hard. you can continue
as if you're no longer on loan, you only have to love.
you only have to let the soft animal of your body love what it loves.

meanwhile in latin.
meanwhile in a hospital gown.
meanwhile at night the body dies.
meanwhile by morning the body is back on shift.
meanwhile you are left sitting alone in a cramped carriage.
meanwhile you extend a smile to a stranger and it ricochets back into
                                                    your face.
meanwhile in exhaustion.
meanwhile in the guardian.
meanwhile the world goes on in despair.

you do not have to be good,
i don't think that's the point anymore.

four

who says you can't get swung on during ramadan

they say i stay sad.   really, i chose to not get got,

grind my teeth, dig my heels/   camp my belongings on the final step, not

inches into the sand, never   retaliate by tongue, but by

coming up for air/ they stole   swords. it's *ramadan*. i rescue

my name; their overusing   my *ibadah*. revise hooks, jabs,

and uppercuts. they left out   the battle of badr/

the part of the story where i   fight/ i water my plants, religiously;

refuse death. they say   maybe i was too harsh.

i was too harsh.   too green and too sad.

frida, lover of womxn

in a whitechapel chicken shop,
bossman gives me two extra wings
and a toothless wink.
i can see into his thoughts:

take a lover
who looks at you
like maybe you are a bourbon biscuit.

he is undressing any woman in his sights.
i wonder if he does that on jummah,
before or after the khutbah.

frida is sat at the next table
with women who look like her
at different ages and a seat just for her sorrow.

she is filing her nails to a stiletto point,
that would prick any man in her way, even iblis.

there is something in the way she rolls up her sleeve,
revealing her scars. she is debating with me
about whose love is worse:

my husband spits i love you's like
flecks of tobacco.

netflix interlude (ii): poem against bingeing

the snack bag for the show,
that was the deal?
now we are neck deep in crumbs
and story lines we were never invested in.

falling just short of a cocktail

how often do you look into yourself?

every night
i turn over and find a carcass in bed with me
wonder what the smell is   put it down
to lack of self-love   like the moon   i have way too
many faces i'm not sure if this is how God intended
me to turn out   but i am sure hooyo wished
she stopped at nine   instead of birthing
this vessel of smoke   here i am   reading
pharmaceutical leaflets   researching what drugs
don't show up on toxicology reports   look
into my wallet   you will find my organ donation card
wrapped in flesh   i do not wait for death to call me
clearly   i am ready now

are you made in god's image dear girl?

if by image you mean bodies lodged
together   like endless umbilical cords
then yes   come to think of it
i'm not sure if i was feeding off him or him off me
do you mean swelling and rising
if by image you mean
my jaw locked in a shape i cannot speak from
or drowning   not knowing life
sitting
turning over the channel
watching another war unfold
then yes
god made me perfectly so

but what does your mother think?

why don't you ask her
she seems to speak easier to people
who aren't her own   don't know if that's because of
colonialism or because you don't resemble
a man   who took so much

all my life   i watched
her contemplate an exit
watched her force feed   him into   forgiveness
imagined him   taking back   his punches and
replacing them with   child support money
so ask her   i dare you

                              what do you do when you're alone?

                                          i aestheticise my scars
                                          pray   for a better time
                          some days   i think of living
                  but fall just short of drowning in a cocktail

a warning to the house that holds us
After Hibaq Osman

i have lived longer than we both expected
but don't remind me of death when i have forgotten its taste.
like thunder on a beach, she sat in a locked room warning me,
the house that holds me. don't be surprised.

don't remind me of death when i have forgotten its taste.
i left behind my papers, reclaimed citizenship,
the house that holds me. don't be surprised
the bricks began to rattle, we tried to delay it.

i left behind my papers, reclaimed citizenship,
the swollen top lip that remained on the stansted coach.
the bricks began to rattle, we tried to delay it,
she tried to warn me but i gave up believing.

the swollen top lip that remained on the stansted coach,
doesn't it taste good?
she tried to warn me but i gave up believing.
if nothing else, i tried.

doesn't it taste good?
isn't it the most perfect salt?
if nothing else, i tried.
i told you not to remind me.

three

moqadishu funk: a history of migration

dur dur first discovered jazz before the war   all saxophones and good vibrations
they say it sounded like the athan   the call to prayer   all intimate they say it
sounded like a pre-wedding night   holy and forbidden   jazz makes the people
electric   before most of the country had electricity
for a while they kept trying to smooth out the creases   like the sound was a fabric
their tendency to make everything flat   but not jazz

.

dur dur flee   some to europe   others from states to states   all away
from home   cassette tapes are buried   along with bodies   *they should never have*
started singing in the first place   all hell breaks loose   the people think
dajjal has arrived   or iblis   they see the moon split like the land
ya'juj and ma'juj   isa descending into damascus   a cloud of smoke
yawm al qiyamah   the day of reckoning   they thought it was iblis
but it was just siad

dur dur are part of the diaspora kids and grandkids   language turns from af
somali to af english   to af dutch back to af somali but by choice this time
maxawees's are ditched   for bootcut jeans hido iyo daqan for mini-skirts and
tube tops   michael and prince are our uncles now   the moon splits again
but this time   it is like a baby opening its eyes to the world

.

dur dur reunite after decades and decades of statelessness   *they should never have*
stopped singing in the first place   all heels are off the floor   all etiquette and shame
out the window   an invasion of colours and silk dresses   free mixing and
twerking   mourning and celebrating   a gift of headwraps   the song talks of
burning ships on lido and berbera   smoke feels like it's at our feet   they sing
about sunsets that actually touch us but feel so distance   they sing about
genocide   grandmothers are at the front of the stage
they are back in 1980s moqadishu   tonight   the songs are
postage stamps commemorating the loss of their country

the only doll i ever owned was torn apart

arms swung back   into a frenzy
two fingers in
            three out   i tally the loss
            of limbs
she never carried   a name on her hip
                         not like
everyone did   she folded
her legs
        under
            herself   sat
longer than anyone has ever sat before
the loss   of sensation
one day   i found her head
meters away   from her torso
mutilated   like the other girls
a   suicide   note
reading   lol

frida camps in a dingy dalston nightclub

she sits at the bar in a grey suit,
her hair slicked back, a tall glass
of dead man in her hand.

i wish i could do whatever i liked
behind the curtain of "madness".

we lock eyes. she runs
her nails across the rim of her glass and
the bartender drops dead.

the man who has been buying her drinks
all night, finds his hand missing in the
buckle of her trousers. blood everywhere.

she walks across the dance floor
ripping through every soul in her way.
she slices a man's neck open with her
martini glass and takes a spleen out
from another.

and they all say: "poor thing, she's crazy!"

netflix interlude (i): poem against season six

take the girl for a second, and unravel the sealed vacuum
bag she is in. rookie mistake. enter a boy
with no plausibility, but for the entertainment of the problem. i can't stand
to see it. write: she should climb mountains she left
behind in season one. write: a kidnapping. write: a framed murder.
write: a broken heart.
how predictable. leave her with an inheritance she deserved originally.
cancel mid-season.

human interactions

she hasn't been home for twenty years.
hasn't crossed borders or rivers, draws
lines between fiction and reality.
airport arrivals grant her more anxiety than departures do.
sometimes, to leave is to stay afloat, is to keep
your head above water and never return.

rivers cross themselves over and over. they hold
loved ones closest. confuse rubber dinghies,
faulty life jackets and new-borns. *what would god think*
about your actions? she, the woman, screams to the ocean.
the ocean, swallows her and spits out *god*
is an immigration lawyer, doesn't want to hear another tragic story.
they, the rivers, work in allegiance to the flag of the deceased.

she, the woman, imagines an ocean not in conflict
with survival. leaves behind her mother, for twenty years.
leaves behind the mountains of sheikh,
the golden sand of the miig, the mediterranean.
builds herself into a bridge,
promises to never allow anyone to die under her or walk over her.

two

frida knows all about men

in the mirror,
i paint a memorial on my face.

frida is on my bed,
an iron cast around her body,
encasing her pain.
her spine is a crumbling column,
her legs dangling like feminism
in front of black women.

there have been two great accidents in my life
one was the train,

she traces her collar bone,
and comes across burn marks
even she is surprised to discover.

the other was diego.
diego was by far the worst.

frida sketches *all my love is unrequited*
across her chest,
a crossbar to the skull.

i uncap my black eyeliner
and write *my therapist knows all about you*
across my eyelids.

we invite men into our homes
and they leave
mud marks on the walls.
they never leave it in the same
state they found it.

fire

they wonder how you made something of yourself.
you told them that you stopped dwelling
on what could have been.

they see you standing in the park
muttering *find me* to pink pigeons and crisp packets,
as if communicating with them was easier
than your family.

they call your speech urban, but
it's scratching at things that shouldn't be
scratched, and when it does, it sounds like
extinguishers crying.

the council flat you were a girl in has had its doors fixed, now
the tenants can sleep with both eyes closed, not
hold your fear of him climbing up you
while you're trying to dream.

they call your dreams urban, but
the doctor who told you that your nineteen-year-old boy
died from a stroke, makes eye contact on the 25 bus.
you cling to your bag,

back in that white ward, that white room,
that white-white moment – and
nod in his direction. get off
before the big sainsbury's, before the station.

they call our love urban, but
you don't cry at your son's funeral,
or on his birthday. no, you mourn
the anniversary of his first football match.

they call our grief urban, but
the man who said he loves you
wraps his arms around the waist of someone
less damaged. you don't care

until you do, until you are
standing outside his house
holding a full glass of water.

examples of confusion

an uncut woman
is not a clean woman,
the nurse translated. meant to say
the doctor needs to open you up,
the stitches were done too tight.
meant to say
everything
will be ok.
but said *ceeb ma lihid*:
don't you have shame?

the scar healed wrong,
layers of skin grew but never closed.

you should feel ashamed
of what they don't know.

he's always on the ward for dying patients.
how does he move past the angel of death each night?

it feels awkward to use my full name.
it's too immigrant to say out loud.
they argued on what to call me,
he wanted a name that i couldn't run away from,
she wanted a three dimensional one.
said i was her luul,
carved and sculpted in the womb, too precious
to let go.

the drive to heathrow was grey.
somehow londoners call this summer,
they don't know that warmth is in colour.

boqoradda caraweelo

caraweelo is crowned.
voice reports ripple across the country,
a woman is now their leader.

the people reject her in unison.
they say they're not ready for a woman,
that she will turn herself into the entire somalia if they let it.
she replies *you were not ready for death either*
or nomadity but now you have found yourself
living amongst both.

it was reported that once,
caraweelo saved an entire village from a lion,
wrestled that mane to the ground.
it was reported that once,
she saved a wife from her husband,
wrestled that mane to the ground.

i worry i planted the idea for castration.
on a monday morning, we follow a beginner's yoga tutorial,
dual mats facing the window.
she glides into the downward dog,
her crown grazing the mat.
caraweelo jokes about suffocating her husband like he was patriarchy.

on the tuesday, like medusa she seduces him.
then leaves his body in uncompromising positions
like stone or yoga, he is in an involuntary headstand.

in burco

the womxn own the markets,
wear sandals two sizes too small,
heels hanging off the edge. baati's peaking below
their jilbabs, a talisman out of its socket.

i don't need to lie about my deen, oh no.
they notice the colour of my aura, a puncture
of red all over the streets. a sealed pocketbook
stuffed below my mus'haf, below my suitcase,
below my infidelity.

auntie in the forest green
rams her wheelbarrow into my bag, the entire
road screams deception and i am back
in siad's regime. *i don't need to lie about my deen.*

in abti's house, three roads north, he holds
tajweed classes in the courtyard. his miniature radio held
close to his ear, enough to tune out the low humming
of boys and girls rocking back and forth to the melody
of Al-Malik's words.

i never speak on the 99 names, for fear of being outcaste,
only able to grasp 22 since 97'.

there is not much of me
in this tuctuc. i am forced to sit in the middle,
flying over bodies that have hardened into road bumps.
whatsapp dial tones continue,
it was only a matter of generations until they found out.

one

origin stories
After Safia Elhillo

depending on who you ask i was made out of clay
or regrets   on the sixth day i was clawing
my way out of the uterus   nearly lost myself before i began
on the sixth night   i pushed us out of bed
into supermarket traffic   kept knocking on the angels' door

depending on who is loudest   i was born trouble or
under a rhyming planet
i slept in a double cot   with an ageing womb
the last of a tribe

depending on which government   i am either six
or sixteen   my birthday is either july 6 or   7

depending on how you   inspect   i am either
breech   or crowning
hanging or   standing
rising   or falling
the start   of peeling a guava   or the end
the fall of man   or the floor

first quarantine with frida kahlo
After Safia Elhillo

all my body is, is bones and ovaries,
walls breaking down.
all my body is, is polio.

i wonder if all breaking feels like this?
if some pains are silent, if some pains are death.
i am so often alone
because i am the person i know best.

it must be somewhere, this right leg,
this right foot. it must move somehow.
all these ribs i cannot reach.

i am 22 and always running,
i've have not yet figured out the direction.
when my shoes wear out,
i run barefoot.
have found thousands of ways to say *tired.*

frida paints herself, herself, herself.
i was born a bitch, i was born a painter.
this is the refrain of her days,

she cannot reach anything.

losing to the cycle of being kind
After Caroline Bird

i do kind gestures   overdose
swallow my pain   i wait for green men
convince my five-year-old niece i'm in her class at school
teach myself long division and cut off crusts
i water plants   overwater plants   give up my seat on the train
terminate life   only walk on the road   ask chicken shop owners how
                                                                        they are
hope for a return   probably get married   open my legs   have a
                                                                        smear test
visit family   attend funerals   say he was a good man
never plagiarise on essays   lie to protect
sit in a pub without drinking
let a man kiss me when i don't want him to
file a police report
take the spider out the bath
hand someone a tissue under a bathroom cubicle
pretend to lip sync   have kids   tell them only the good things
tie my tubes   brunch   make conversation at school gates   brunch
get divorced   brunch   move house   brunch   fix broken window
brunch   maybe not overdose again brunch
sneak in at 4am   brunch
my mission is over
i do good deeds

days of future

the first time my brother saw a white man,
he asked me if this is what death looked like.
never again questioned the existence of ghosts.

i heard shame. thought
it sounded like my mother
but according to my brother shame is all women.
shame must stop speaking.

do you remember when we danced on the moon?
the interlude sounded better with
disco lights screaming. we ran at command.
i lost my footing and fell into the hole,
you came back for me.

my mother found mouldy dishes under my brother's bed,
how long have they been there?
somewhere between three months
and not breathing.

i don't know when this ache began,

maybe when you threw me your love
and i didn't catch it
or when you left without warning.

there's something you should know,

it takes a lot to love someone by obligation.
to want their suffering to end at your expense,
the first time I felt this my father had his fourth stroke.

my mothers' kitchen bench

after my neighbours janazah, my mother distributes her home.
scatters the memories across charity stores and to her children,
leaves a single item for herself: an adjustable bench.

the angle of the sun predicts where to find my mother. it is after asr,
she is preparing dinner for the ones who've left. our love language
is taking turns, one managing the fire, the other holding a weapon.

cut the onions slices smaller. when are you moving back?

she is sitting on her bench, i wonder if it can tell between lovers.
since the breakup, several screws are loose, the arm rests
have anxiety punctures and the legs need adjusting.

one day, it'll leave her for another fling. this heartbreak may
be my inheritance. i tell her i can manage standing, in fact
i'd prefer to not sit on death whilst holding a weapon.

ode to east london

After Sumia Jaama

to roman road, to bow.
to grime and dizzee rascal.
to tinchy pulling up outside mums.
to cfgs and st luis.
to the boys outside the betting shop.
to the ones who stayed past their non-existent curfew.
to the kids who were never allowed to be kids.
to the blockbusters.
to al huda and prank calling the imams.
to internet cafes and phone cards.
to talk home and talk direct.
to the hair shop before the costas.
to everything before the costas and the prets.
to stratford centre and new look.
to 32aa bras.
to e1, e2, e3, e15, ec1.
to the staircase in bethnal green.
to the big sainsbury's and aisle 13.
to the corner i first got stood up at.
to first kisses in playgrounds.
to brick lane and the taste of coffee before oat, soya, almond.
to climbing into victoria park after hours.
to passing that dutch.
to discovering boys.
to missy elliott telling me to avoid the pretty ones.
to hand-me-down adidas and fila.
to mile end.

Acknowledgments

It is incredibly surreal and humbling that this pamphlet is making it out into the world. I never thought I'd want to be a writer, poet, author or all that comes under this but I've been lucky enough to be supported by an incredible amount of people. To show gratitude is to say, I did not arrive to this place by myself. All praise is for Allah, to whom we belong and to whom we return.

I want to thank two of the most influential mentors and facilitators I've had. Jacob Sam-La Rose and Rachel Long. Jacob, thank you for letting me onto the Barbican Young Poets programme and for allowing me to believe in my voice. Rachel, I cannot thank you enough for your support and guidance, for Octavia – the sisters in writing I never knew I needed – and for all you stand for. Thank you to the poetry community within BYP, Octavia and more, I may not have continued to write without you all.

To Yomi, you didn't know me enough to give me the opportunities you did, but you offered that support to me as an investment and out of kindness. I hope I've made you proud. To BoxedIn, always to BoxedIn. To Natalie, Sean, Cecilia, Abu and Juliet, thank you for letting me grow at my own pace.

I couldn't have got here without Suhaiymah, your intelligence and kindness has gotten me through so much. Thank you to you and Faye for creating a beautiful home that allowed me to be safe enough to write and share. To all my friends who've helped me work through imposter syndrome and more. To Ibtisam, Hadia, Bayan, Sumia.

To my family. Always my family. My siblings and nieces and nephews, I pray we grow as a unit and I continue to love you all on and off the page. Sophia, Yasmin and Sado, specifically, your unspoken support gets me through a lot. To Mohamed, for being a light and for being more like a brother than a nephew.

To Ayeeyo Halimo, for being the reason I write. To Aabo for providing me with all the skills I've ever needed and for being the first supporter I ever had, may you rest in peace. Lastly, to my mum. Hooyo Macaan. Everything I do is for you. I love you in this life and in the next.

glossary

- Hooyo – Mother
- Qalbiyaay toos – My heart, wake up
- Haba Suud – Black Seed Oil
- Buur – Mountain
- Janazah – Funeral Prayer
- Astagfirullah – I seek forgiveness in Allah (God)
- Qiblah - the direction of the Kaaba (the sacred building at Mecca), to which Muslims turn at prayer
- Ramadan – Holy month in Islam
- Ibadah - Worship
- Jummah – Friday congregational prayer
- Kutbah - Sermon
- Dajjal – Evil figure in Islam
- Iblis – An angel who did not prostrate to God
- Ya'juj and Ma'juj – Gog and Magog are angels
- Yawm al qiyamah – The day of resurrection/ reckoning
- Caraweelo – Queen of Somalia in 14AD
- Baati – Pajama dress
- Jilbab – A full length outer garment covering head and hands
- Mus-haf – A collection of the Quran (Holy Book in Islam)
- Abti – Uncle
- Tajweed – A set of rules governing the way the Quran should be recited
- Al-Malik – 'The king of king': one of the 99 names and attributes of Allah